I0190315

Apprentice Lessons

Apprentice Lessons
Copyright © 2015 Thom Brucie

All rights reserved.

No part of this publication may be reproduced
or used in any form or by any means without
permission of the author except for quotations
embodied in critical articles and reviews.

Printed in the United States of America and
committed to the standards set by the Green
Press Initiative.

Cover Design – Carol Brucie
Photos © Carol Brucie

Daniel's Vision Press – 2015
ISBN-13: 978-0-9887094-2-3

Grateful acknowledgment is made to the
journals in which the following poems first
appeared:

"Legacy" ("A Carpenter's Legacy")
 appeared in
The Dead Mule School of Southern Literature

"A Carpenter's Eye"
appeared in
Wilderness House Literary Review

For Virgil McLynn

Whose word needed no contract;
Whose hands mastered form;
Whose care for others
    exceeded the care he devoted to craft.

I have filled him with the Spirit of God,
to design artistic works,
and to work in all manner
of workmanship.

Exodus 31: 3-5

Apprentice Lessons

a chapbook of poems

*   *   *   *   *   *   *   *

Thom Brucie

TABLE OF CONTENTS

APPRENTICE LESSONS

Apprentice: What is craft?
Virgil: Knowledge applied to function and form.

Apprentice: What is art?
Virgil: Craft that displays beauty.

Apprentice: What, then, is beauty?
Virgil: Beauty reveals the mysterious unity of all things.

LEGACY

Virgil always signed his work.
Somewhere hidden in a wall
or the back of a cabinet
we signed our names and left the date
so one day another carpenter
would find us,
and we would pass our legacy
to another generation.

He wanted everything we built to last
one hundred years.
Some of my early work
stood on sand; some constructed in weeds;
only after many indignities of carelessness
did I learn
to seek foundations of granite
and attention to time.

I look back upon the number of my days,
the walls I stood,
the roofs I framed;
I have spent the expanse of my body
in making things,
calling forth structure from wood and steel,
amassing a fortune of memories,
making cabinets, doors,
windows, floors,
walls and ceilings.

Do these monuments, the heartwood of my craft,
justify my energy?
I wonder for those who sleep
under the roofs I built.
Are they dry? And safe?
The foundations of my family, deep and robust?
Are the walls of my friendships plumb?
What is my life made from
if not the corridors I have built
between my burdens and my loves?

A CARPENTER'S EYE

Virgil said
a good carpenter always stands back
and looks at his work.
He made me stop often,
and I resented his interruptions,
for I did not need to take a rest
and call it looking.

One day
I watched the lines of two walls
meet in a perpendicular,
and my vision grew acute,
like a plumb-bob and a level.
I saw with the eye of a carpenter,
the eye of tension and forgiveness.
Virgil taught that if a wall is
already out of plumb,
build the new wall to match it,
and no one looking at the new work
will recognize either imperfection.

The blemishes of this world
call unto themselves –
lies, greed, betrayal;
but the attributes of daily bread
need no headlines,
for the aim of the eye is truth,
not judgment,
and caution reminds us
that we do not always stand plumb.

AN HONEST DAY'S WORK

Pope John Paul made the edict:
An honest day's work for an honest day's pay.
Virgil approached work
neither from a profit-driven attitude
nor from philosophic design.
He told me –
If you don't like the work you do,
find a new job.

A man's true work
revels in joy,
it surpasses dollars
with esteem,
and it allows God to display His reality
in beauty.

If a man produces beauty
with his handiwork,
that is reason enough
to get out of bed
every morning,
and sleep serves recuperation
not escape.

HANDS

Hands compel the imagination
to accept form;
they bring forth balance
between thought and dream;
hands lure vision into substance.

Virgil called hands
tools of the toolmaker.
All hands are good,
he said,
but some are better than others.

PAYDAY

The first payday,
after he counted out my cash,
eighty-seven dollars and thirty-nine cents,
Virgil handed me a 12-point Sandvik
cross-cut saw.

Back then,
before the days of conglomeration,
they made worthy saws,
balanced, with comfortable apple wood grips
set with four brass screws.

He told me that when I could cut
a straight line
with the hand saw,
at a 90 degree angle,
then I could use a power saw.

Two months later,
he presented me a hand auger with five balanced bits.
He told me that when I could drill a hole
perpendicular and straight,
then I could use a power drill.

He told me to accumulate tools,
and like habits,
if I chose good ones,
they would sustain desire
and accrue good results.

THE CHISEL

The first chisel Virgil bought me
measured an inch across,
thick, flat, and sharp as flint-glass,
for cutting wood at areas
where I could not squeeze a saw.
Later, I bought a half-inch chisel,
razor thin and precise,
its fine edge sharp as a line of silver fire.

The chisel holds stout
under the hammer blow
and cuts an artistic ravine
as cedar, fir, alder, and ash
curl in obedience to its
formidable authority.

The chisel holds its place in the toolbox quietly,
resting in the excess
of chalk and saw dust,
out of the way of screw drivers and
the cat's paw,
never complaining at difficulty of effort
nor at its limited access to fame.

SANDPAPER

Sandpaper moderates uneven surfaces
and eases hard edges
to make the denseness of wood
feel soft.
Sandpaper raises the luster of irregular grain
and peels away skin-thin layers of rough surface
to reveal the inner beauty
of the species.

Like the chisel, sandpaper is designed
to discipline matter
in man's declaration over nature.
Adam began it, this need to control,
by naming things,
and since,
every individual
has measured his life
by the application of will to obstacle.

THE FRAMING SQUARE

When Prometheus tricked Zeus
into demanding as offering
the uneatable innards of a calf,
leaving the sweetness of meat for human benefit,
Zeus grumbled.
When Prometheus tricked Zeus
into releasing flame from the burning sun,
and he brought fire to humankind's hearth,
Zeus threw lightning bolts of rage.
But when Prometheus tricked Zeus
into revealing the secrets of the framing square,
Zeus commanded Prometheus
into the darkest corner of Tartarus,
for the square divulges the mysteries
of algebra and geometry
on hash marks along two metal bars
joined at a right angle.
It releases the enchantment of gables and gambrels,
domes and dormers,
hips and valleys,
designed from encoded mathematics,
and fashioned into patterns,
each dazzlingly unique,
each an independent self,
like each son, each daughter.

SHARPENING THE CLAWS OF THE HAMMER

Virgil taught me to sharpen the straight claws
of the framing hammer
with tiny grinding circles
and short strokes,
into the nail groove
and along the edges,
turning the metal gray with tough Arkansas stone,
raising its luster with soft India whetstone.

Properly swung, the framing claws,
like a saber-toothed ax,
split the width of man-milled wood
as they strike along the grain.
With dedicated practice,
you can make the pieces dance,
and the music of the hammer-sting rising into trees
rustles leaves the same way wind does,
invisibly, secretly,
like wood calling to wood
in distant times.

.

A HICKORY HAMMER HANDLE

Hickory makes the best hammer handle.
The handle is eased
from the heart of the hewn giant
whose beauty is as obvious in its height
as in its color.
The wood, smooth and dense,
absorbs each strike,
taking the shock upon itself,
away from callused palm and brittle wrist.

Like a human body, a hickory shows
its age with scars
and brags of youthful energy
in supple boughs.
It gives hope
that the individuality we demand of trees
may fall to us as well.
Yet, like the hands that fell it,
the hickory finds in its time, dust.

I am not always certain
that my days on earth will amount to memory
beyond my own,
but I hold the secret prayer that
my daughters and my sons might endure
as I will not,
that wisdom pass to them
as sap to leaf.

BENT NAILS

The trick to pulling nails
lies in the angle of the claw.
Hook the claw onto the nail
and bend it sideways,
one way, then the other,
and the nail comes out,
a little at a time,
without breaking the hammer handle.
The bending and pulling
crooks the nails into geometric shapes
unsuitable for use.
Virgil made me straighten them.

Bent nails move with serpentine irregularity,
and you cannot straighten a bent nail
with one swing;
you correct one flaw and
move to the next,
one swing of the hammer at a time.

Early on, I hit my finger
more than I hit the nail.
I learned to look only at one kink at a time,
and hit it.
I learned, eventually, to keep my fingers
out of my own way,
and I learned to strike the nail square on,
like any other matter of concern.

15

HINGES

We hung doors with thick, rectangular hinges,
balanced,
holding thirty-seven times their weight.
Heavy with strain and time,
hinges hold a household's secrets
within the soundless judgment
of lock and key.
Solid and firm within the jamb,
quietly moving silent slabs of wood
open and closed,
hinges throw open the doors of hope
and shut in the forlorn shroud of shadowed solitude.
We needless trust what truths
both come and go.

THE SMELL OF ASPHALT

Virgil got a job repairing the roof
of an old manufacturing plant.
I worked the melted asphalt.
It was summer, in the fierce days of my teens,
and I walked a line of 55 gallon drums
cut in half the long way, placed end to end
in three rows.

Under each row, propane pipes held fire
against the belly of the barrels.
I released the hard cakes
from their cardboard girdles
and watched them swell
into popping black smudge-bubbles
as I stirred the murky butter with a metal flat bar,
releasing lava smoke of deep oil pitch.
Each long day of watchfulness and sweat,
mixing the glue that held the hot patches,
I trailed back and forth
within the ghostly steam,
the stench of it working itself into my nostrils
and into my throat, like boiled camphor.

Now, I can smell the labor of men in asphalt
a mile away if the wind is right,
and I remember the difference
between the hot and the cool of effort.

WITCHING FOR WATER

The driller parked his rig
along the roughed-out driveway
and pulled the witching stick
from behind the seat,
a barkless Y,
stained the colors of hand sweat and tannin.
"It must be oak, and it must be native," he said.

He held it waist high
and pointed the tip away from him
toward the yellow grass
of the back acres.
He walked until the tip pulled
toward the earth
and into the dusty weeds.
He drove a nail in the spot,
set the rig, hit the spot with the drill bit,
and brought in 21 gallons a minute at 148 feet.

I thought the stick held a charm,
or the well-man knew a chant,
but Virgil had seen it all before,
watched nature offer itself for use,
known men who trusted tradition over technology.
He never doubted we'd find water;
nature conjures its own magic.

STONEWORK

Virgil favored natural stone,
paralleling a wall,
cushioning a column,
adorning each effort
with colors of harvested earth,
each slice of mountain
revealing edges of umber and pyrite,
blue-stone and onyx.

Stonework does not recognize obtuse corners,
cannot comprehend meaningless endings.
The mass settles into appreciable moments
of permanence,
like the inert pressure of tradition.
Nothing superfluous
measures like the intense perspective
of length, width, and depth,
so that the energy of timelessness makes time stop.

The numbness of copied repetition flees
when a stone monument intercedes
on behalf of stucco and paint,
and we, mortared to the ordinary,
are set free in its ferocity.

THE MATHEMATICS OF ENCHANTMENT

A 3-foot by 4-foot by 5-foot triangle
makes a right angle.
This knowledge allows the builder to carry
a straight line
along and away from an already existing point
in space and time.
The line, if extended, has two options –
if the universe is flat, like the earth,
the line will extend to the end of eternity;
if it is flexible, and self-contained,
like an Einsteinian glass ball
resting on the back of a turtle,
the line will continue in an ever-lasting 180 degree angle,
and eventually return upon itself.

The elegance of mathematics,
its geometric subtlety
of right angles and straight lines,
can connect a room addition to a house
and a straight line to the universe.
The thunderous accuracy of mathematics
suggests that a house is more than an angle and a line,
more than mortar and brick,
more than foundation and roof.

If properly constructed,
a house becomes its own universe,
the beginning and end
of memories scratched in the table top,
and growth charts on the wall;
of holding fast to grandma's stew recipe,
and the crawling stage of granddaughter's daughter;
of summers running out the back screen-door,
and of all things stored in three-dimensional boxes,
and stories,
and hearts.

A STRONG FOUNDATION

Virgil ordered the cement truck too early.
It looked like storm,
birds warbling and scurrying in the mist,
a sure sign.

The truck arrived,
and then the rain.
He guided the chute through it,
but the heavy concrete rushed
and collapsed a brace weakened in the mud.
He drove his shoulder
against the breach,
and the effort strained his heart.

The chute flew wild,
and concrete hurried
to a meaningless pile.
He fell into a concrete splatter
when he dropped.

The heart attack softened his ambition
and brought to focus
each thin moment of every startling day.
Two weeks later,
while I jack-hammered spilled concrete,
the sun fell warm on my neck,
Virgil rested in the shade,
and two mated mud-ducks swam nearby.

GOD

Virgil believed in God.
He would raise his Norse eyes to the sky
and say,
"He who looks beyond the vast blue
must see eternity."

I sometimes shrugged at his imagery;
I did not trust his vision then.
Death, failure, and forgiveness
had not yet imparted wisdom to me.
"One day," he promised.

CONFESSION

I confess
that I have added to the burden
of the earth,
for I have plastered
with smooth trowel and clever design
concrete suffocation
over much soil.

No one made me.
I did it for money.
I accepted gratuity from those who
drove prosperity
in order to fatten my wallet.
I did not think of polar bears
or indigenous peoples.
I thought about food
and rent
and steel-toed boots.

For penance
I shall plant one more tree
five more flowers
ten blades more of grass
each spring, before I die;
I shall hold hope as a deterrent to commerce,
and nature as a measure for art.

WHEN VIRGIL DIED

He is not dead to me.
He will live one hundred years,
his memory as solid
as any wall we framed.
The care of trees
and respect for beauty
he passed to my hands.

I cannot accept a shoddy cut
or a miter that's off one degree.
Cuts and miters and the care of others
must be exact.

We bury the bodies of those we love;
we must.
Perhaps it is necessary that
each generation die
in order that we may look to them
to know the evil in the world
is balanced by their good.

VIRGIL'S WIFE

Virgil's wife, Bridgett,
wore her hair
in two long yellow braids.
She had a soft chin
and kind eyes like hillside lilacs.

She wore an apron when she cooked.
She baked fruit pies,
and sometimes sent one to us
with a sliver of chocolate or cheese.

Bridgett rose early every morning
to cook breakfast and pack his lunch.
At evening she prepared
meat and bread and two glasses of iced water.

After the funeral
I asked,
"Need anything?"

"No," she said. "I am surrounded
by what he made,
and the things he made
remember him."

Am I not also one that he made?
Shall I not then become thus to another?

Photo by Carol Brucie

The poems in Thom Brucie's *Apprentice Lessons* focus on the dignity revealed in those daily moments of human effort we sometimes perceive as common, and yet which suggest by their shared importance that each individual life emits the power of everlasting relevance.

His other works include the poetry chapbook, *Moments Around The Campfire With A Vietnam Vet*; a collection of short stories, *Still Waters: Five Stories*; and the novel, *Weapons of Cain*.

www.thombrucie.com

www.ingramcontent.com/pod-product-compliance
Lightning Source LLC
Chambersburg PA
CBHW060042040426
42331CB00032B/2240